MEN FACING TEMPTATION

llace

12 studies for
individuals or groups

CREATED MALE & FEMALE BIBLE STUDIES

*With Study Notes & Guidelines
for Leaders*

INTERVARSITY PRESS
DOWNERS GROVE, ILLINOIS 60515

InterVarsity Press® is the book-publishing division of InterVarsity Christian Fellowship®, a student movement active on campus at hundreds of universities, colleges and schools of nursing in the United States of America, and a member movement of the International Fellowship of Evangelical Students. For information about local and regional activities, write Public Relations Dept., InterVarsity Christian Fellowship, 6400 Schroeder Rd., P.O. Box 7895, Madison, WI 53707-7895.

All Scripture quotations, unless otherwise indicated, are from the HOLY BIBLE, NEW INTERNATIONAL VERSION®. NIV®. Copyright ©1973, 1978, 1984 by International Bible Society. Used by permission of Zondervan Publishing House. All rights reserved.

Cover photograph: Michael Goss

ISBN 0-8308-1137-0

Printed in the United States of America ∞

15	14	13	12	11	10	9	8	7	6	5	4	3	2	1
03	02	01	00	99	98	97	96	95	94	93				

Getting the Most out of Created Male & Female Bible Studies

Created Male and Female Bible Studies are designed to help us understand what it means to be created in the image of God. We know that God had a purpose in creating two sexes. Discovering gender distinctions is an exciting and intriguing part of what it means to be human. But sometimes it is confusing and frustrating as well. These studies will help us understand what God's purpose is for us individually and as a part of the human race.

The passages you will study will be challenging, inspiring and practical. They will show you how to think about your sexuality and how you live that out. And they will help you to better understand what the other sex is about—breaking down stereotypes and helping you find new ways to communicate.

These guides are not designed merely to convince you of the truthfulness of some idea held by the authors. Rather, they are intended to guide you into discovering biblical truths that will renew your heart and mind. How? Through an inductive approach to Bible study. Rather than simply telling you what they believe, the authors will lead you to discover what the Bible says about a particular topic through a series of questions. These studies will help you to think about the meaning of the passage so that you can truly understand what the biblical writer intended to say.

Additionally, these studies are personal. At the end of each study, you'll be given an opportunity to make a commitment to respond—to take steps toward changing the way you think and act. And you'll find guidance for prayer as well.

Finally, these studies are versatile. They are designed for student, professional, neighborhood and/or church groups. They are also effective for individual study.

How They're Put Together

Created Male and Female Bible Studies have a distinctive workbook format with space for writing a response to each question. This format is ideal for personal study and allows group members to prepare in advance for the discussion or write down notes during the study. Each study takes about forty-five minutes in a group setting or thirty minutes in personal study—unless you choose to take more time.

At the end of the guide are some study notes. They do not give "the answers," but they do provide additional background information on certain questions to help you through the difficult spots. In addition, the "Guidelines for Leaders" section describes how to lead a group discussion, gives helpful tips on group dynamics and suggests ways to deal with problems which may arise during the discussion. With such helps, someone with little or no experience can lead an effective group study.

Suggestions for Individual Study

1. As you begin the study, pray that God will help you understand the passage and apply it to your life. Ask him to show you what kinds of action to take as a result of your time of study.

2. In your first session take time to read the introduction to the entire guide. This will orient you to the subject at hand and to the author's goals for the studies.

3. Read the short introduction to the study.

4. Read and reread the suggested Bible passage to familiarize yourself with it.

5. A good modern translation of the Bible will give you the most help. The New International Version, the New American Standard Bible and the New Revised Standard Version are all recommended. The questions in this guide are based on the New International Version.

6. Use the space provided to jot your answers to the questions. This will help you express your understanding of the passage clearly.

7. Take time with the final questions and the "Respond" section in each study to commit yourself to action and/or a change in attitude. You may wish to find a study partner to discuss your insights with, one who will keep you accountable for the commitments you make.

Suggestions for Members of a Group Study

1. Come to the study prepared. Follow the suggestions for individual study mentioned above. You will find that careful preparation will greatly enrich your time spent in group discussion.

2. Be willing to participate in the discussion. The leader of your group will not be lecturing. Instead, he or she will be encouraging the members of the group to discuss what they have learned. The leader will be asking the questions that are found in this guide.

3. Stick to the topic being discussed. Your answers should be based on the verses which are the focus of the discussion.

4. Be sensitive to the other members of the group. Listen attentively when they describe what they have learned. You may be surprised by their insights! When possible, link what you say to the comments of others. Also, be affirming whenever you can. This will encourage some of the more hesitant members of the group to participate.

5. Be careful not to dominate the discussion. We are sometimes so eager to express our thoughts that we leave too little opportunity for others to respond. By all means participate! But allow others to do so as well.

6. Expect God to teach you through the passage being discussed and through the other members of the group. Pray that you will have an enjoyable and profitable time together, but also that as a result of the study you will find ways you can take action individually and/or as a group.

7. Be ready to make a personal application of the principles in the study. The final questions will guide you in this. Although you may or may not wish to discuss the "Respond" section as a group, you may want to hold one another accountable in some way for those personal commitments.
8. We recommend that groups agree to follow a few basic guidelines, and that these be read at the beginning of the first session. You may wish to adapt the following guidelines to your situation:

☐ Anything personal which is shared in the group is considered confidential and will not be discussed outside the group unless specific permission is given to do so.

☐ We will provide time for each person present to talk if he or she feels comfortable doing so.

☐ We will talk about ourselves and our own situations, avoiding conversation about other people.

☐ We will listen attentively to each other.

☐ We will be very cautious about giving advice.

☐ We will pray for each other.

If you are the group leader, you will find additional suggestions at the back of the guide.

How the Series Works

Where should you start? If you'd like to go through several guides in the series, whether with a group or individually, a good place to start is *Sexual Wholeness*. This guide will give you a good overview of the issues, and you may find various areas you want to explore further. While *Sexual Wholeness* may be used in either same-sex or mixed (male and female) groups, it may be uncomfortable for some in mixed groups. As a companion to that guide, you may wish to use *Created for Relationships*. If you are in a mixed group, this may be a more comfortable starting place.

Created Female and *Created Male* are designed for same-sex groups but could be used together for enlightening discussions in mixed groups. To facilitate this use, studies three through five are the same in both guides. The other studies could be intermixed so that group members have a unique opportunity to hear the perspective, needs and struggles of the other sex.

Women Facing Temptation and *Men Facing Temptation* are also designed for same-sex groups but could be adapted for use in mixed groups. You will find that all the temptations covered are applicable to either gender. This could be an opportunity for interesting discussion about how these temptations are both similar and distinct for each sex. You may discover new ways to support each other and help one another avoid temptation.

For two quarters of study on how we live out our gender roles, *Roles in Ministry* and *Following God Together* make good study companions. *Roles in Ministry* looks specifically at the role of women in the church by studying the relevant passages and is designed to help the reader find a unique place of service. Through a series of character studies involving pairs of men and women, *Following God Together* will help us see the temptations and frustrations men and women find in service together and the great possibilities for ministry when abilities are combined.

Introducing *Men Facing Temptation*

When my wife learned that I would be working on a Bible study guide concerning temptations which males commonly confront, she asked me two questions that got me thinking.

The first was, "What makes these studies particularly fit *men?*" As you work through this guide, it is important to note that the temptations studied are by no means exclusive to the male gender. Nor do the topics exhaust the list of temptations that men face daily. However, these particular temptations are typical for men in our culture. Our society defines success, manhood and strength in such a way as to push men toward these temptations and sins.

The second question my wife asked was, "So where are you going to do your research?" I jokingly told her that there was none needed. "When it comes to temptations, I'm my own case study." All of the topics presented here are issues that I have faced personally, some far more than others. Some of these studies will "hit home" with you more than others. Let me encourage you to look at each temptation with the degree of seriousness it deserves but to protect yourself from seeing sin where none really exists. Ask God to give you the proper perspective.

In each study you are asked to think deeply about your own character and actions. Introspection may not come naturally to you, but stick with it. The Lord will expose what is needed as you think and pray. And sharing these things with one or more trusted friends can lead to healing and growth.

My hope in these studies, however, is that you won't stop with mere introspection. Each study will ask you to develop practical strategies for change. Be careful not to merely establish new *laws*. Develop helpful means of fighting your particular temptations, given your particular personality. Lofty goals and strategies can produce frustration and unwarranted guilt, so be practical and realistic.

One last thought. Our ability to name our temptations and take practical steps to avoid falling into sin is an important part of every Christian's walk with Christ. However, only Jesus and the abiding presence of the Holy Spirit can bring real purity and sanctification. We must put our trust in Christ for lasting change in our character and behavior.

May God use this guide to develop your love for Jesus and your Christlikeness of heart.

Brian M. Wallace

1
Jesus Our Model

Matthew 4:1-11

I have often had the privilege of listening to people share their particular struggles against sin in their walk with Christ. I am always struck by the depth of their honesty and integrity. It is difficult to admit your sin to another person.

I am also struck by the almost universal sense of aloneness my friends feel. The shame and discouragement resulting from their sin are compounded by a sense that they are the only one in their fellowship or church who struggles in such a way. I will never forget the look of relief on one friend's face when he found out that he wasn't the only Christian who wrestled with certain sins. Far from encouraging him to sin more, our sharing provided this man (and everyone else present) with new resolve to *resist* temptation.

Open
☐ How have you been able to help someone, or has someone been able to help you, after learning of common struggles or problems?

☐ How do you usually respond when confronted with temptations in your life?

Study

Read Matthew 4:1-11. (To best grasp the passage, read it carefully and slowly at least two times. This will help you get the most out of the study.)

1. What were the issues behind each of the three temptations that confronted Jesus? What actions were encouraged and what rewards were promised?

2. How might these rewards have been particularly tempting to Jesus at the outset of his public ministry?

3. In what ways are you susceptible to each of the temptations with which the devil confronted Jesus?

4. Why did Jesus go into the desert (v. 1), and what does this reveal about the nature of his tempting?

5. Why was it important that Jesus be tempted? What purpose did it play in his life and ministry? What good came of it?

6. What are some possible purposes of temptation in our lives? How does it help us grow?

7. How does Jesus' understanding of your temptation—because he himself has been through it—encourage you in your walk with Christ?

8. What were the resources available to Jesus as he fought against his temptations?

9. Spend some time identifying the resources God has provided to help you in your struggles against the temptation to sin. How can you make better use of these resources? What can you do now to prepare yourself to face temptation in the future?

Respond
What are some of the ways members of your church or fellowship encourage one another to resist temptation? What practical step can you take this week to to encourage or empower a friend in his struggle against sin?

2
Tempted to Be Independent

Feb 13/96.

Genesis 3:1-7

*A*s a child I was forever wishing to be older than I was. I wanted to be as old as my brother and sisters. It appeared to me that they got to do what they wanted. They could stay up as late as they liked. Their freedom seemed as limitless as my restrictions.

I have now come to understand that my desire for age was really a desire for a level of independence which my parents wisely deemed inappropriate for my youth.

Nothing seems to have changed. Even now I struggle against the "restrictions" which the Lord has given me for my own good. This wrestling against the rules, the desire to be free of restriction, the insistence on being in control of our own lives, is a part of all of us. It is part of our inheritance. And it can lead to sin.

Open
☐ When in your youth did you find it difficult to submit to an authority figure?

☐ Do you find it easier to lead and be in control or to be led? Why?

Study
Read Genesis 3:1-7 at least a couple of times.
1. What is the progression of the serpent's temptation of Eve? What is his strategy against her?

2. Identify Eve's resistance and lack of resistance to the serpent's suggestions.

3. What eventually causes Eve to do what God has instructed her not to do? (Note: The rest of this chapter makes it clear that Adam shared equal responsibility with Eve.)

4. What do you think Eve thought it meant to "be like God"?

5. In what ways, if any, is the desire to be like God a temptation for you?

6. In what ways are you tempted to be independent of God? Be specific.

7. Part of the reason Eve gave in to the temptation to disobey God was that she began to believe some of the lies the serpent was telling her. To what degree are you susceptible to believing some of the same lies?

8. What are some truths that you could remind yourself of when you are tempted to disobey God and/or be independent of him?

9. In what ways have God's standards or restrictions on your behavior worked in your life for your good?

Respond
What evidence is there that someone in your circle of friends is struggling with an unhealthy level of independence? What can or should be done? What steps can you take?

3
Tempted to Compete

Genesis 4:1-8

*O*ne of the most exciting things in spectator sports is to see athletes perform their best under the pressure of big events like the last inning of the World Series or the last minute of the NBA finals. Yet competition can have the opposite effect as well. A person may consistently swish baskets from twenty feet in practice and not be able even to hit the rim during the game. Competition can bring out the best or worst in our performance. It can also bring out the best and often the worst in our character.

During a recent family holiday, my three-year-old son and his four-year-old cousin were almost inseparable for four straight days. For the most part they got along great. However, each was forever trying to beat the other. "I have three Happy Meal ducks and you only have two!"

Many of us have learned to compete with one another from childhood, even when no competitive situation is apparent.

Open
☐ How does the presence of competition affect your performance in sports, business or recreation activities you enjoy?

☐ As you grew up, were you encouraged to be competitive? How?

Study

Carefully read Genesis 4:1-8.

1. In what situation does Cain find himself? How does it make him feel and act (vv. 3-5)?

2. Why does God accept Abel's sacrifice, but not look with favor on Cain's? (Consider the descriptions of the offerings.)

3. The presentation of offerings to God is not a naturally competitive activity. What does Cain's treating it as such (and his subsequent angry reaction) tell us about his motives?

4. What competitive situations do you tend to handle poorly? Why?

How does this show up in your emotions and/or actions?

5. In what situations, if any, do you create competition where none naturally exists? Why?

What does this expose about you either positively or negatively?

6. Cain's anger eventually causes him to take his brother's life. What do you feel toward others while you are competing, and how does it affect your relationships with them?

7. What is God's counsel in response to Cain's anger (v. 6)? With what does God want Cain to be concerned? Does Cain listen?

8. How can the counsel Cain received help us deal with potentially competitive situations?

Respond
How can you or those in your circle foster an atmosphere free of unhealthy competition? As you go through this week, note the times that you are tempted to be overly competitive or to create competitive situations. How does this affect your relationships?

4
Tempted to Perform

Matthew 6:1-18

Look, Mom, no hands!" From an early age we develop a capacity to perform for the people whom we love and who are important in our lives. There is something about hearing your dad say, "Good catch, way to go!" or, "That's a great picture of an elephant." Those achievements in our lives are motivating and encouraging. They keep us trying.

However, our need to perform, be it for ourselves, other people or even God, can become unbalanced. I remember a reading contest held by my first-grade class. I "won." Well . . . I didn't really read more books than the others, but it was so important for me to be noticed that I lied.

Open

☐ What are some of the times in your life when you performed well? How did it make you feel?

☐ Have there ever been moments in your life when the pressure to perform or to live up to other people's expectations moved you to behave in a way you knew was wrong?

Study
Read Matthew 6:1-18.
1. List the external acts of "righteousness" mentioned in this passage.

2. What about these acts makes them particularly hypocritical?

3. What unifying instruction does Jesus give concerning acts of righteousness? Why?

4. What is the reward for hypocrisy mentioned in verses 2, 5 and 16?

What does this look like in both our culture and our church environment?

5. Jesus offers a true reward in verses 4, 6 and 18. What do you think it is?

6. In Matthew 5:16 Jesus charges his disciples to "let your light shine before men, that they may see your good deeds and praise your Father in heaven." How is this different from the public displays of righteousness listed in chapter 6?

7. How important to you is the approval or praise of other people? How does the need for approval show itself in your day-to-day affairs?

8. What truth from this passage might help you deal with this need in a healthier way?

9. Spend some time in prayer, confessing yur sins before the Lord and thanking him for his love and his forgiveness of your wrong motives.

Respond

This week, determine to look back at the end of each day and assess whether you acted in hypocrisy at any point in order to receive approval or avoid disapproval. Talk it over with another person if possible. As you notice the ways in which you "perform," try to begin to be more genuinely yourself—and to look more to Jesus, not people, for acceptance.

5
Tempted to Wield Power

Mark 10:35-45

*P*atton, Roosevelt, Stalin, Hitler, Kennedy, Gorbachev, Moe Turrentine, David Bowen, Dick Wallace. They all are or were leaders, be it of nations, armies, movements, classrooms, churches or families. Some leaders have used their position wisely and for the common good.

Unfortunately, power has corrupted some. Most of our lives have been touched by it in some way—a teacher, administrator, athletic coach or parent who has used authority inappropriately. It makes us angry, and rightly so. But it would be foolish of us not to begin to recognize some of these tendencies in our own lives as well.

Open
☐ How would you define *leadership?* What are the marks of an effective leader?

☐ Think of one individual whose leadership you have appreciated and one whose leadership you have *not* appreciated. What characterizes their leadership styles?

Study
Read Mark 10:35-45 very carefully.
1. Briefly retell the conversation recorded in this passage.

2. Why did James and John ask to sit one on Jesus' left and one on his right? What did they really want?

3. What was James and John's strategy for securing a positive response from Jesus?

4. A new word was coined recently for someone who hovers close to a famous person whenever a photo opportunity presents itself: *Velcroid.* What are some other ways in which people in our society posture or position themselves around people in leadership? Give an example.

5. What positions of status or authority, if any, do you desire to attain or have you desired at some point? Why?

What have you done to attain them?

6. Jesus seizes a potentially explosive situation among his disciples to teach them something about the godly use of position, power and authority. Summarize his teaching by comparing and contrasting the two styles of leadership presented.

7. What are some examples of the subtle ways we in our culture use position to "lord it over" others? Suggest examples from both secular and church settings.

8. What positions of leadership or authority do you hold now, and how are you tempted to use your position inappropriately?

9. In what ways is Jesus a model for us in servant leadership?

10. What are some practical ways you could serve people in your circle of friends or sphere of influence?

Respond
Scripture tells us that leadership is God-ordained and important. Experience tells us that leaders often face special temptation or attack. Make a list of your main spiritual and secular leaders. What are some difficulties that they may be facing? How can you best serve them and pray for them? Determine to do something this week.

6
Tempted to Abuse Money

Luke 12:13-21

I was driving down the road one afternoon and heard a commercial that started me daydreaming. The radio station was holding a contest worth ten thousand dollars. *What would I do with ten thousand dollars?* I wondered. As my mind tossed around all the exciting options, it occurred to me that one could do much more with twenty thousand dollars than with ten. Before I realized what I was doing, I was planning what I would do with a hundred thousand dollars!

Relating this story to my family and friends made me realize that I am not alone. It seems that winning the lottery has become the new American dream. However, my normalcy is hardly comforting. This incident awoke me to the reality that there is at least a small part of my character that could never win, earn or have enough money.

Open
☐ In regard to your financial "health," would you say you are as strong

as an athlete, in good health but needing more exercise, suffering a bad cold, or terminally ill?

☐ Take a brief inventory of your financial and material world. What are the main riches God has given you?

Study
Read Luke 12:13-21 at least twice.
1. What is the setting or occasion that prompts Jesus to tell this parable?

2. Define the word *greed.* What are some different ways greed can manifest itself in our society?

3. In what ways does greed show itself in your own life and attitudes?

4. As you read through the parable, take note of the pronouns used. For what or for whom is the rich man concerned?

5. What behaviors or attitudes does Jesus condemn in this parable? Explain.

In telling this parable, is Jesus saying that ownership of money and possessions is wrong?

Why or why not?

6. From the teaching in this passage, what should our attitude toward our money be?

What role should it play in our relationship with God?

with people?

7. To what extent do you worry about money or financial well-being?

8. In what ways are you tempted to put your security in your possessions or money?

9. Spend some time thanking God for his provision in your life, committing your possessions to God's control and asking him to provide for your needs.

Respond

Over the next week, it may be helpful to talk with your family or a friend about your money. Ask some good questions: Am I storing things up for myself or am I saving wisely; am I giving enough away; do I trust God to take care of me financially?

It may be helpful to read and think about Jesus' teaching immediately following this parable—see Luke 12:22-34.

7
Tempted to Be Driven

Mark 1:29-39

*B*usyness has become a high virtue in modern American culture. Many of us run our lives by our appointment calendars, frantically scheduling and rescheduling our time. We have come to believe that a busy life is a successful life and that a life filled with activity is an important life.

In *Ordering Your Private World,* Gordon MacDonald points out that our activity may be a drive to succeed or achieve rather than an attempt to obey God's calling on our lives. Many of us are driven people, not called people.

In this study we will look at how Jesus deals with an unusually busy schedule and how he handles the pressures of "success."

Open
☐ What makes you, or would make you, feel like a success?

☐ Describe the top of your desk or the back seat of your car. What does their condition reveal about (a) your personality and (b) your schedule?

Study
Slowly read Mark 1:29-39.
1. Describe the scene at Simon and Andrew's home.

2. What clues from this passage indicate an unusual amount of activity for Jesus?

3. Why are people looking for Jesus (v. 37)? What does this tell you about Jesus' level of popularity or success in Capernaum?

4. How might Jesus have been tempted to stay in Capernaum?

5. What motivates Jesus to move away from Capernaum to other villages?

How does he come to his decision?

6. What does your daily schedule reveal about you and your priorities or goals?

7. Consider the time and place of Jesus' prayer life in this passage. What does Jesus' example teach concerning the practice of spiritual disciplines in the setting of our daily schedules and life goals?

8. How does a particularly busy day affect your spiritual disciplines and your walk with Christ?

9. Jesus left Capernaum in obedience to God's call and purpose for his life. What steps are you taking or do you need to take to obey God's call on your life?

Respond
To what degree is your schedule out of line with your spiritual and familial priorities? What are the symptoms of stress in your life? Think about corrective steps you need to take to recapture your schedule for Christ. Share them with a close friend and ask for input and prayer.

8
Tempted to Keep Emotional Distance

Luke 7:36-50

*I*f you watch any television at all, you have seen this picture a number of times. A teenage boy plays as hard as he can in his chosen sport while his father, burly and gruff, sits stoically in the stands. As the boy and his father meet after the game, they give each other a long stare, and the father finally gives a nod of approval, maybe a handshake or even a hug.

This type of scene touches a chord in many men. We so desperately need to know what our fathers feel about us. As little boys and as young men we needed to receive that nod or touch that meant, "I love you; I'm proud of you."

I feel very fortunate that my father was the type of man who was willing to touch me comfortingly and speak words of love and reassurance when I needed them.

Sadly, many men have grown up without that assurance because their fathers were not able to give it. The small yet meaningful displays of emotion were forbidden by a never-spoken but widely held false definition of manhood.

Open

☐ As you were growing up, what were the spoken and unspoken lessons you learned about manhood?

☐ In what ways are you like your father in regard to your emotions and their expression?

Study

Read Luke 7:36-50.

1. Detail the emotions Simon the Pharisee seems to be having and how he does or doesn't express them.

2. Given the setting and her known history, what emotions do you think the woman is having? How does she express them?

3. What are the reasons this passage gives for the woman's emotion?

4. What is Jesus' response to the woman? How does he seem to feel about her emotional display?

5. With regard to your feelings and their expression, with whom do you more readily identify, Simon or the woman? Why?

6. In what situations do you feel hesitant to communicate your feelings? Why?

What emotions do you feel free to share, and why?

7. Of what have you been forgiven, and how do you communicate your emotions of thanks and love to the Lord?

8. Spend some time thanking God for what he has done for you, and asking him to help you grow in thankfulness and love.

Respond

As you go through this week, think of one or two ways you can communicate your feelings of love, gratitude or intimacy with the special people in your life. Then do it.

If you are like many others, you sometimes have difficulty identifying your emotions. It may help to keep a journal of your feelings and thoughts. Writing things down when you are unsure about how you feel can often make them much clearer, as well as helping you articulate your feelings at a later time.

9
Tempted to Abuse Sexuality

Matthew 5:27-30

Sex is an important part of who we are. Indeed, God created us as sexual beings, and our sexuality is part of what God called *good.* However, sex has become an overly important part of our world. It motivates, it sells, it entices us relentlessly. As a society, we have come to take it for granted. "What could be more normal?" we ask.

In the wake of Magic Johnson's disclosure of having contracted the HIV virus in the fall of 1991, we began to hear of his and other sports and entertainment celebrities' staggering sexual exploits. As a society, we didn't question that right away. "It's only natural," we said. "It's all part of being a man." Out of our collective shock and respect for Magic, it was a few weeks before the country could begin to question the morality of a promiscuous lifestyle.

Living as a part of our culture sometimes has an unconscious effect on our thinking. Unbridled sexuality has become so "normal" that we may have begun to take our own sexuality lightly.

Open
☐ What do you think is the prevailing attitude of the people in your community toward sex and sexuality? What role does it play in their lives?

☐ What sexual attitudes or behaviors fit into your understanding of *right?* of *wrong?*

Study
Read Matthew 5:27-30 several times carefully.
1. What is adultery? What do you think it really means to "look at a woman lustfully"?

2. Look back to verses 17-20, where Jesus sets the stage for the following teachings. Why do you think Jesus redefines what it means to commit adultery?

3. Given Jesus' new definition of adultery, what are some attitudes, actions or behaviors which are seen as acceptable by our society but which Jesus considers wrong?

4. In addition to the fact that Jesus declares them adultery, why are these behaviors wrong? How are they harmful?

5. According to this passage, what is the consequence of adultery as Jesus defines it?

6. What does this passage say we must do in response to our sexual temptation? What do you think it means practically?

7. If Jesus is not to be taken literally here (vv. 29-30), why do you think he uses such graphic imagery?

8. What, if any, are some of your attitudes, actions and behaviors that Jesus would call adulterous? What steps should you take in light of this?

Response
In order to make yourself more aware of how you are tempted, make note this week of every advertisement, situation or activity that tempts you to commit adultery in your heart. (This would be a good activity to do with some other men so you can talk about it at the end of the week.)

10
Facing Temptation

Genesis 39:1-12

*B*eer, automobiles, sports equipment, after-shave, shirts, chewing gum, razor blades—what do these have in common? All of them, and more, are sold to us by the use of sexually suggestive images or themes. For those of us who struggle against sexual temptation, it is difficult to live in our culture without facing temptation regularly—for some, it seems, every moment! All of us face regular temptation of one sort or another, be it deceit, greed, hatred or sex.

Serious temptation exists for all of us. The difference between holiness and sin will be determined by the way we respond to the temptations as they come.

Open
☐ Other than in advertising, what are some of the ways sexual temptation confronts us in our culture?

☐ What are some other temptations you run into in your day-to-day living (work, school, family . . .)?

☐ Is it wrong to be tempted? Why or why not?

Study

Carefully read Genesis 39:1-12.

1. In this story we tend to see Joseph as the tempted one and Potiphar's wife as the temptress. However, we can't overlook the fact that Potiphar's wife was faced with a strong temptation herself. What was the nature of her temptation?

2. How did Potiphar's wife deal with the temptation? What could she/should she have done?

3. What was the nature of the temptation Joseph faced? Detail in your own words its severity and regularity.

4. What, if any, temptations which you face are similar in nature to those faced by Potiphar's wife (a constant, passive presence in her life), and by Joseph (an aggressive, daily confrontation)?

5. Which type of temptation is more difficult for you to combat, and why?

6. What steps did Joseph take to protect himself (and Potiphar's wife as well) from temptation?

7. In the temptations you face, what are some initial steps of protection or caution that you are taking or could take?

8. What reasons did Joseph give for not going to bed with his master's wife? What should be our motivation for fleeing temptation?

9. In verses 11-12, the situation becomes volatile. Joseph is prevented from performing his duties. And then fleeing temptation costs him his job and ultimately lands him in prison. At what point could the situations of temptation you face become equally explosive, and what are some of the potential costs in fleeing temptation and pursuing holiness?

10. Spend some time asking God to give you both the strength and the willingness to resist the temptations in your life.

Respond
Ultimately, temptation is a spiritual battle. Spend daily time this week thanking God for the way he has protected you in the past, and pray, "Lead me not into temptation, but deliver me from evil."

You may find it helpful to spend a week identifying the consistent temptations built into your daily life. Discuss with a friend the best strategies for coping with them.

11
A Sure Forgiveness

1 John 1:5—2:2

As a college sophomore, I was startled to find myself dealing with my sin and the overwhelming sense of guilt I had by writing a check to a local Christian charity. "What am I doing?" I thought. "Am I trying to buy God's forgiveness?"

As I looked over my Christian life, I found that this wasn't the first time I had tried to make amends for my sin and assuage my guilt with some act of service. Now, eleven years later, I can see that I was operating under some terrible misconceptions about God's love and forgiveness. I thought that if I really loved Jesus, I wouldn't continue to sin. And if I did, I should pay.

My sins are no less wrong now than they were eleven years ago, yet the Lord has taught me the truth about the nature of forgiveness and about what my responsibility is when confronted by sin. The truth has set me free.

Open
☐ What are your common emotions when confronted with your sin? What do you usually do first?

☐ How easy or difficult is it for you to receive forgiveness from other people? from God?

Study
Read 1 John 1:5—2:2.
1. Identify everything this passage teaches concerning the presence of sin in the lives of true believers.

2. In light of this teaching on sin in our lives, what does John mean by "walking in darkness"? (Provide both a definition and an example.)

3. From this passage, identify appropriate attitudes toward our sin and its presence in our lives.

4. What action does this passage instruct us to take in response to our sin?

What response from God is promised?

5. Besides confession, what else is needed to secure God's righteousness in our lives?

What has Jesus done on our behalf, as identified in this passage?

6. How do you need to grow or change in order to respond biblically to the awareness of sin in your life?

7. What particular encouragement do you find in this passage?

8. If you have not already done so today, spend some time in confession and praise to God.

Respond

Spend time identifying some of the inappropriate ways you have responded to the presence of sin in your life. What do you think encouraged you to respond in the ways you have? Talk with the Lord about all this.

You may want to memorize 1 John 1:9 or some other verse that assures you of God's love and forgiveness.

12
A Power to Change

2 Thessalonians 2:13-17

*I*t is always encouraging to hear the testimony of a person who has come to Christ out of a sordid background to experience a radically changed life. God can and does break addictions, heal relationships and restore our priorities.

However, for most of us, growing into the image of Christ is a less dramatic process involving lots of prayer, struggle and frustration. A string of broken promises I made to God about sin while in high school prompted me to ask some questions which I've since learned are common among young believers: *Why do I keep doing what I don't want to do? When will I ever stop? How can I change?*

Open
☐ What are a couple of areas of struggle that have persisted throughout your Christian walk? Why?

Study

Read 2 Thessalonians 2:13-17 a couple of times.

1. From this passage, identify how the Thessalonians came to faith in Christ.

What was God's role?

What was the role of the authors of this letter (Paul, Silas and Timothy)?

2. Through what is salvation secured (v. 13)?

3. What is God's specific role or activity in our sanctification—the event and process of being made to conform to God's character and holiness (vv. 13, 17)?

4. What commands does this passage give to believers?

What does it reveal concerning *our* responsibility in the process of sanctification?

5. From what we learn in this passage, how do Christians grow and change?

6. What patterns or practices have you developed which are helping you "stand firm and hold to the teachings"?

7. How did Paul, Silas and Timothy aid in the spiritual growth/sanctification of the believers in Thessalonica?

8. What people or resources are in place to help you in your Christian walk and in the process of becoming more Christlike, and and how can you better take advantage of them?

9. Read through this passage again and make note of all God's work on our behalf.

Then identify specific ways God has changed you (your character, attitudes or behavior) since you committed your life to him. In order to celebrate and remember God's work on their behalf, the people of Israel often erected altars or monuments. These specific evidences of God working in your life can serve as monuments of God's love for you. Spend some time meditating on the list, thanking him for his work in your life.

Respond
Look back at question 6. Can you see a new pattern or practice which you need to develop, in order to hold to the teachings and grow in personal holiness? Decide how you will begin working at it this week.

Guidelines for Leaders

Leading a Bible discussion can be an enjoyable and rewarding experience. But it can also be intimidating—especially if you've never done it
before. If this is how you feel, you're in good company.

Remember when God asked Moses to lead the Israelites out of Egypt?
Moses replied, "O Lord, please send someone else to do it" (Exodus
4:13). But God gave Moses the help (human and divine) he needed to
be a strong leader.

Leading a Bible discussion is not difficult if you follow certain
guidelines. You don't need to be an expert on the Bible or a trained
teacher. The suggestions listed below can help you to effectively fulfill
your role as leader—and enjoy doing it.

Preparing for the Study

1. As you study the passage ahead of time, ask God to help you
understand it and apply it in your own life. Unless this happens, you
will not be prepared to lead others. Pray too for the various members
of the group. Ask God to open your hearts to the message of his Word
and motivate you to action.

2. Read the introduction to the entire guide to get an overview of the
subject at hand and the issues which will be explored.

3. Be ready for the "Open" questions with a personal story or example.

The group will be only as vulnerable and open as its leader.

4. As you begin preparing for each study, read and reread the assigned Bible passage to familiarize yourself with it.

5. This study guide is based on the New International Version of the Bible. It will help you and the group if you use this translation as the basis for your study and discussion.

6. Carefully work through each question in the study. Spend time in meditation and reflection as you consider how to respond.

7. Write your thoughts and responses in the space provided in the study guide. This will help you to express your understanding of the passage clearly.

8. It might help you to have a Bible dictionary handy. Use it to look up any unfamiliar words, names or places. (For additional help on how to study a passage, see chapter five of *Leading Bible Discussions*, IVP.)

9. Take the final (application) questions and the "Respond" portion of each study seriously. Consider what this means for your life—what changes you may need to make in your lifestyle and/or actions you can take in your church or with people you know. Remember that the group will follow your lead in responding to the studies.

Leading the Study

1. Be sure everyone in your group has a study guide and Bible. Encourage the group to prepare beforehand for each discussion by reading the introduction to the guide and by working through the questions in the study.

2. At the beginning of your first time together, explain that these studies are meant to be discussions, not lectures. Encourage the members of the group to participate. However, do not put pressure on those who may be hesitant to speak during the first few sessions.

3. Begin the study on time. Open with prayer, asking God to help the group understand and apply the passage.

4. Have a group member read the introductory paragraph at the beginning of the discussion. This will remind the group of the topic of the study.

5. Every study begins with a section called "Open." These "approach" questions are meant to be asked before the passage is read. They are important for several reasons.

First, there is always a stiffness that needs to be overcome before people will begin to talk openly. A good question will break the ice.

Second, most people will have lots of different things going on in their minds (dinner, an exam, an important meeting coming up, how to get the car fixed) that have nothing to do with the study. A creative question will get their attention and draw them into the discussion.

Third, approach questions can reveal where our thoughts or feelings need to be transformed by Scripture. That is why it is especially important not to read the passage before the approach question is asked. The passage will tend to color the honest reactions people would otherwise give, because they feel they are supposed to think the way the Bible does.

6. Have a group member read aloud the passage to be studied.

7. As you ask the questions, keep in mind that they are designed to be used just as they are written. You may simply read them aloud. Or you may prefer to express them in your own words.

There may be times when it is appropriate to deviate from the study guide. For example, a question may already have been answered. If so, move on to the next question. Or someone may raise an important question not covered in the guide. Take time to discuss it, but try to keep the group from going off on tangents.

8. Avoid answering your own questions. Repeat or rephrase them if necessary until they are clearly understood. An eager group quickly becomes passive and silent if members think the leader will give all the "right" answers.

9. Don't be afraid of silence. People may need time to think about the question before formulating their answers.

10. Don't be content with just one answer. Ask "What do the rest of you think?" or "Anything else?" until several people have given answers to a question.

11. Acknowledge all contributions. Be affirming whenever possible. Never reject an answer. If it is clearly off base, ask "Which verse led you to that conclusion?" or "What do the rest of you think?"

12. Don't expect every answer to be addressed to you, even though this will probably happen at first. As group members become more at ease, they will begin to truly interact with each other. This is one sign of healthy discussion.

13. Don't be afraid of controversy. It can be stimulating! If you don't resolve an issue completely, don't be frustrated. Move on and keep it in mind for later. A subsequent study may solve the problem.

14. Periodically summarize what the group has said about the passage. This helps to draw together the various ideas mentioned and gives continuity to the study. But don't preach.

15. Don't skip over the application questions at the end of each study. It's important that we each apply the message of the passage to ourselves in a specific way. Be willing to get things started by describing how you have been affected by the study.

Depending on the makeup of your group and the length of time you've been together, you may or may not want to discuss the "Respond" section. If not, allow the group to read it and reflect on it silently. Encourage members to make specific commitments and to write them in their study guide. Ask them the following week how they did with their commitments.

16. Conclude your time together with conversational prayer. Ask for God's help in following through on the commitments you've made.

17. End on time.

Many more suggestions and helps are found in *The Big Book on Small Groups, Small Group Leaders' Handbook* and *Good Things Come in Small Groups* (IVP). Reading through one of these books would be worth your time.

Study Notes

A word to leaders: As you consider leading these studies in the context of a group, please keep in mind the very delicate nature of the subject. Temptation and sin are both grave and intensely personal. Use appropriate caution when asking folks to share their struggles and temptations. Protect each member's dignity by realizing the guilt and shame that may accompany their answers to the questions.

Some of the "Open" questions that begin each study may be inappropriate for general discussion in your group. In these cases, encourage members to take a couple of minutes for private reflection.

If, however, your group has been together for a long time and has already enjoyed a deep level of openness, you may want to seize the opportunity these studies provide for greater accountability and prayer for one another. Consider using some of the "Respond" suggestions for this purpose as well.

Study 1. Jesus Our Model. Matthew 4:1-11.

Purpose: To explore the purpose of temptations in our lives and recognize and begin to employ some of the tools available to us for fighting temptation.

Questions 4-6. Notice that Jesus was "led by the Spirit into the desert to be tempted" (v. 1). The Spirit had some purpose in mind for allowing this tempting. "On the one hand, temptation signifies any attempt to entice into evil; on the other hand, temptation indicates a testing which aims at spiritual good" (*The New Compact Bible Dictionary*, ed. T. Alton Bryant [Grand Rapids, Mich.: Zondervan, 1979], p. 579). Clearly Satan tries to entice Jesus into evil, but to no avail. Therefore, "because [Jesus] suffered when he was tempted, he is able to help those who are being tempted" (Hebrews 2:18). "For we do not have a high priest who is unable to sympathize with our weaknesses, but we have one who has been tempted in every way, just as we are—yet was without sin" (Hebrews 4:15).

Question 9. It is significant that Jesus faced his tempter each time with Scripture. (Yet we cannot forget that Satan himself proclaimed "for it is written" [v. 6]. We need to take pains to understand Scripture properly and never to twist it to our own devices.) The Spirit of God led Jesus into the desert and presumably remained there with him as a comfort and aid. Note that angels came to minister to Jesus after the devil left.

Study 2. Tempted to Be Independent. Genesis 3:1-7.

Purpose: To explore the sinfully independent nature that is a part of all of us as we inherited it from Adam.

Question 1. First, he questions whether God really provided the commandment: "Did God really say . . . ?" Second, he tells Eve a lie and questions God's intentions toward them (v. 4).

Question 3. In verse 6 we are told that Eve sees two things that move her to take the fruit. First, the fruit appears tasty and looks attractive—enticement for tongue and eye. Second, she desires the "wisdom" that will make her "like God."

Question 7. Note that Eve was not in trouble until the lies the serpent told caused her to question the validity of God's commandments and to doubt God's good motives.

Question 8. God's rules or restrictions on our behavior are there *for our good,* just as one might put a leash on a dog to prevent him from running into a busy street. God loves us and cares for us as his children.

Study 3. Tempted to Compete. Genesis 4:1-8.

Purpose: To examine our wrongly competitive tendencies and to consider practical steps to combat sinful competition in our lives.

Question 2. "The contrast is not between an offering of plant life and an offering of animal life, but between a careless, thoughtless offering and a choice, generous offering. Motivation and heart attitude are all-important" (*The NIV Study Bible,* Kenneth Barker, gen. ed. [Grand Rapids, Mich.: Zondervan, 1985], p. 11).

Question 6. While it is doubtful that any of us have been tempted to take someone's life as a result of competition, Jesus makes it clear in Matthew 5:21-24 that our anger against others is tantamount to murder, and that we should be quick to reconcile any broken or strained relationships.

Question 7. In verses 6-7 God is asking Cain to focus his attention and desire on doing what is right before God. The Lord promises that if Cain's heart is set on pleasing God, he too will be accepted. He also provides him clear warning not to continue in his jealousy and anger.

Study 4. Tempted to Perform. Matthew 6:1-18.

Purpose: To explore the ways we desire the praise of other people, and why.

Question 2. The acts themselves are good things to do. However, it is clear that the acts of righteousness are performed more for an earthly audience that a heavenly audience. The desired goal appears to be the praise of other people. As John Stott writes, "Behind their piety lurked their pride. What they really wanted was applause. They got it. 'They have received their reward in full' (NIV)" (John R. W. Stott, *The Message of the Sermon on the Mount* [Downers Grove, Ill.: InterVarsity Press, 1978], p. 133). Good acts done for bad motives are not pleasing to the Lord.

Question 5. The rewards offered to us in Christ are in part a promise for the future (the assurance of eternal salvation) and in part for today. The false rewards mentioned here refer to the present—public acclaim and applause. No amount of pious activity will win us the reward of heaven (Ephesians 2:8). In this passage Jesus condemns religious activity for the sake of public approval. He encourages us to seek the appropriate reward that comes from quiet giving, private prayer and fasting—relief for the needy and communion with God. In *The Message of the Sermon on the Mount* (p. 132) Stott writes the following concerning the reward for giving.

> What, then, is the "reward" which the heavenly Father gives the secret giver? It is neither public nor necessarily future. It is probably the only reward which genuine love wants when making a gift to the needy, namely to see the need relieved. When through his gifts the hungry are fed, the naked clothed, the sick healed, the oppressed freed and the lost saved, the love which prompted the gift is satisfied. Such love (which is God's own love expressed through man) brings with it its own secret joys, and desires no other reward.

Question 6. There is a profound difference in letting my Christlikeness shine so that God will be praised and performing my acts of "righteousness" before people so that I will be praised. The difference is, to whom does the praise return?

Question 8. Many of us are tempted to perform "spiritually" for others in order to prove the reality of our own faith experience. Two things may help. The first is a clear understanding of the unconditional nature of our acceptance before God in Christ. The second is the importance of refusing to continue making ourselves the center of our own existence. Stott writes (p. 140), "It is not men with whom the hypocrite is obsessed, but himself. . . . The remedy then is obvious. We have to become so conscious of God that we cease to be self-conscious."

Study 5. Tempted to Wield Power. Mark 10:35-45.

Purpose: To consider the extent to which we seek position and are tempted to abuse power, and to develop a biblical view of leadership.

Question 2. James and John, like the other disciples, probably understood Jesus to be the Messiah who would restore the political nation of Israel and bring freedom from the Roman oppressors. They thought Jesus' rise to glory was imminent; their request was that they share in it.

Question 3. It is a bit manipulative to ask for an affirmative response to a request before making the request! (Note in Matthew 20:20 that James and John's mother seems to be with them and even to make the actual request.)

Question 6. The explosive situation was that "the other ten disciples were indignant because they were jealous of their own dignity and fearful lest the two brothers should secure some advantage over them" (William L. Lane, *The Gospel of Mark* [Grand Rapids, Mich.: Eerdmans, 1974], p. 382).

People in leadership have the opportunity to use their position to serve others or to be served by them. Jesus calls his disciples to follow his own example. He calls us all to use what position and authority we have, not only for our own good, but for the good of others.

Question 10. If you are leading a group through this study, be sure that you leave adequate time to be extremely specific with this question. It may be helpful to spend time planning a service activity for your fellowship group to do together.

Study 6. Tempted to Abuse Money. Luke 12:13-21.

Purpose: To consider the proper place of financial/material resources in our lives and to explore our current attitudes toward our money.

Take special care as you lead a discussion of this passage. Money is difficult to talk about; many people consider their finances and their stewardship a very private matter. Those with more financial resources may feel defensive or guilty, and those without may feel resentful. Still, it's important to make the basic principles clear. Each group member can then apply them to his own life—privately if necessary.

Question 2. In verse 15, some translations render *greed* as *covetousness*. Greed can take many forms; we can desire many things beyond money (position, power, the favor of others).

Question 5. Jesus is not declaring the mere ownership of money or things to be wrong in itself. In the parable, the rich man uses his possessions to prepare for his future on earth, yet makes no provision for his future beyond this life. All things have their proper place. Money should not take such priority in our lives that we lose sight of our eternal relationship with God. Money and possessions must never surpass the Lord in importance in our lives.

Study 7. Tempted to Be Driven. Mark 1:29-39.

Purpose: To find out what our schedules reveal concerning our priorities and our calling, and to study Jesus' example to see how he was truly called and not driven. (We want to learn to not be driven by our goals but to let our goals be driven by our Lord.)

Question 2. The fact that some people waited to come to the house until after sunset indicates that this was probably the sabbath. Hebrew law would forbid them from carrying their sick or healing minor illnesses until after the sabbath, which ended at sundown. Note too that (without the benefits of modern lighting) a normal day's activity generally ended at sundown, with the new day beginning at dawn. On this occasion Jesus stayed up late and got up early.

Question 3. By human standards, Jesus had attained a large measure of success. The whole town knew of him. However, the reason for his huge and growing popularity was that the people were intrigued by the apparent miracle worker in their town and they wanted healing.

Question 5. Jesus, out of care and compassion, used his power to give healing and comfort to those in need. But Scripture makes it clear that healing was not the reason for his incarnation. Jesus had come to preach a message of repentance and faith (Mark 1:14-15). Despite his apparent popularity in Capernaum, Jesus knew that to stay true to his purpose and calling, he needed to move on to other towns to preach there as well: "For that is why I have come" (Mark 1:38).

Question 7. It is unfortunate that the busier we become, the less concerned we are for our personal time with the Lord. Jesus demonstrates for us that we must do whatever it takes to protect our private prayer times. For it is in prayer that we give God our attention so that he can sharpen us spiritually and remind us of his priorities for us. When we say, "I'm too busy to pray," we are asking for trouble.

Study 8. Tempted to Keep Emotional Distance. Luke 7:36-50.

Purpose: To explore our perceptions of "manhood" and how they encourage or inhibit the expression of emotions, and to consider how a biblical self-understanding can help us feel and express emotions appropriately.

Note: The emotions displayed by the woman in this passage are not being held up as a model. Some of our personalities may not allow for emotions to be expressed so openly and passionately. However, we all have deep emotions, and this study tries to help unlock some of those biblically.

Question 2. It was not uncommon for other people to be in the room while some were sharing a meal. The occasion was less a time for eating than a forum for discussion and fellowship. Remember that people of this culture reclined rather than sat; they rested their weight on one arm before a low table (or no table at all) with their legs lying to one side, pointing away from the table.

Study 9. Tempted to Abuse Sexuality. Matthew 5:27-30.
Purpose: To think about the seriousness of sexual sin and consider practical measures to protect ourselves from falling into temptation.

Question 1. For the biblical injunction against adultery see Deuteronomy 19:21. Jesus is not forbidding us to look at women. He forbids lust. Any prolonged looking at women or photographic images, involving the sexual imagination, qualifies as lust. And Jesus equates the mental activity of lusting with the physical activity of committing adultery!

Question 2. To exceed the outward righteousness of the scribes and the Pharisees seemed impossible. They were precise in every detail of the law. Jesus is urging us to understand righteousness in a new way. Righteousness is far less a matter of what we do and don't do than it is the attitudes and motives of our hearts.

Question 4. To think of members of the opposite sex solely as objects of physical desire undermines the nature of their creation. Men and women are creatures of God, created in his image, to be respected, protected and loved. When we *use* another person, we sin against him or her.

Questions 6-7. "The command to get rid of troublesome eyes, hands and feet is an example of our Lord's use of dramatic figures of speech. What he was advocating was not a literal physical self-maiming, but a ruthless moral self-denial. Not mutilation but mortification is the path of holiness he taught, and 'mortification' or 'taking up the cross' to follow Christ means to reject sinful practices so resolutely that we die to them or put them to death" (John R. W. Stott, *The Message of the Sermon on the Mount*, p. 89). Jesus is calling us to take drastic measures against our sin. Sexual immorality has eternal consequences in our lives. It is better to sacrifice our pleasure today than to die eternally.

Study 10. Facing Temptation. Genesis 39:1-12.
Purpose: To identify the presence of temptation in our daily living and to consider protective strategies we can use.
Question 1. "Joseph was well-built and handsome" (v. 6); he was successful; he was right there in her house. What a temptation for Potiphar's wife! We cannot think that men are the only ones who struggle against sexual lust. It appears that Potiphar may have given his wife little attention, thus fueling her desire for Joseph.
Question 2. In group discussion don't get bogged down in the minute details of "could have" and "should have." The intent of the question is to begin thinking practically about avoiding temptation.
Question 8. Joseph was determined to honor his master and the trust his master had put in him. If Joseph sinned against Potiphar, his sin would ultimately have been against the Lord himself, as is any of our sins.

Study 11. A Sure Forgiveness. 1 John 1:5—2:2.
Purpose: To consider appropriate and biblical attitudes and actions in response to the presence of sin in our lives.
Question 1. At first reading, it is tempting to understand verse 7 to mean that if we are truly walking with Christ, we will be free from all sin. But verse 8 tells us the opposite: "If we claim to be without sin, we deceive ourselves and the truth is not in us." If we are honest with ourselves, we will admit that we are daily in a battle against sin. There

is no complete freedom from our sinful nature this side of heaven. Plumbing the depths of the sin in our lives, though frustrating and painful, provides us the opportunity to scale the height of God's loving grace.

Question 2. If the presence of sin in the lives of believers is a reality, then occasional sin by those who earnestly struggle against it cannot be understood to be "walking in darkness." To walk in darkness is to continually choose to hold an attitude or action that we know is wrong, without repentance, and without attempting to resist the temptation to sin.

Question 3. It is important to note that while this passage recognizes the reality of sin in the lives of true believers—and encourages us with the hope and promise of forgiveness—it by no means condones sin. Indeed, John writes, "My dear children, I write this to you so that you will not sin" (2:1). Provided with a sure forgiveness for our failures, we should strive all the more to keep our minds and bodies from sin.

Question 4. It is significant here that John prescribes one action for the assurance of forgiveness in our lives: confession. Many Christians struggle with feeling that they need to perform some service that will make restitution or prove the sincerity of their sorrow. Certainly, one who steals money should return the money if truly repentant. However, it is crucial to know that our outward acts of regret or restitution in no way secure our forgiveness. We are forgiven and made pure only through confessing our sins and putting our trust in the atoning sacrifice of Christ on the cross. (See Ephesians 2:1-10.)

Study 12. A Power to Change. 2 Thessalonians 2:13-17.

Purpose: To consider how lasting change is made in the lives of believers, and to identify our responsibility in the process.

Question 3. Sanctification is both the event and the process of being made to conform to God's character and holiness. It is an event in that when we put our faith in Christ and confess our sins, the atoning work of Christ on the cross purifies us from all unrighteousness. In that instant we are "counted as righteous," seen as sinless and therefore able to stand in the presence of God. However, after we are saved, our life on earth is marked by continued growth and by the ongoing process of being sanctified (made holy). And it is God himself who promises to make us into new creatures in Christ. He encourages and strengthens us (v. 17) as we gradually grow in godliness.

Question 4. We cannot sanctify ourselves; it is the work of God. When we "stand firm and hold to the teachings" (v. 15), we are cooperating with God's sanctifying work in us. Our responsibility in Christ is to stand firm by resisting temptation and holding firm to the truth of the church, resisting the lies of those who would deceive. The *teachings* mentioned here are the traditions of the early church as they were taught by the apostles and later written down in the Scriptures. As we strive to prevent sin and deception from creeping into our lives, the Spirit is at work bringing change.

Question 5. It is impossible for us to achieve lasting change or godliness in our lives independent of the power of God himself. Only God can bring the permanent change that begins when he creates in us "a new heart." It is God's promise to make us new creatures in Christ. Our responsibility is to constantly make our hearts and lives available to the power of the Holy Spirit: to resist temptation, to protect ourselves from deception, to grow in our understanding of the Word of God. Our spiritual disciplines are performed not in order to attain our forgiveness in Christ but in order to remain in fellowship with him. Our efforts to fight against temptation and sin are not the acts through which we are made holy, but the means by which we make ourselves available to the sanctifying work of God.